Explorers of

Vasco Núñez de Balboa

and the Discovery of the South Sea

Explorers of New Worlds

Vasco Núñez de Balboa

and the Discovery of the South Sea

Hal Marcovitz

Chelsea House Publishers
Philadelphia

Prepared for Chelsea House Publishers by:
OTTN Publishing, Stockton, N.J.

CHELSEA HOUSE PUBLISHERS
Editor in Chief: Sally Cheney
Associate Editor in Chief: Kim Shinners
Production Manager: Pamela Loos
Art Director: Sara Davis
Director of Photography: Judy L. Hasday
Project Editors: LeeAnne Gelletly, Brian Baughan
Series Designer: Keith Trego

First Printing
1 3 5 7 9 8 6 4 2

Library of Congress Cataloging-in-Publication Data

Marcovitz, Hal.
Vasco Núñez de Balboa and the discovery of the South
    Sea / Hal Marcovitz.
        p. cm.–(Explorers of new worlds)
Includes bibliographical references and index.
ISBN 0-7910-6428-X (hardcover : alk. paper) –
ISBN 0-7910-6429-8 (pbk. : alk. paper)
1. Balboa, Vasco Núñez de, 1475-1519–Juvenile
literature. 2. Explorers–America–Biography–Juvenile
literature. 3. Explorers–Spain–Biography–Juvenile
literature. 4. America–Discovery and exploration–
Spanish–Juvenile literature. 5. Caribbean Area–
Discovery and exploration–Spanish–Juvenile literature.
6. Pacific Ocean–Discovery and exploration–Spanish–
Juvenile literature. [1. Balboa, Vasco Núñez de, 1475-
1519. 2. Explorers. 3. America–Discovery and
exploration–Spanish.] I. Title. II. Series.

E125.B2 M35 2001
973.1'6'092–dc21
[B]   2001028272

Contents

Stowaway

In 1510, a Spaniard named Vasco Núñez de Balboa (inset) stowed away in a ship that was headed to Central America. In the unexplored jungle, Balboa hoped to find fame and fortune.

I

On one warm morning in September 1510, a ship was preparing to leave Santo Domingo, a bustling seaport on the island of Hispaniola in the Caribbean Sea. Commanding the ship was Martín Fernández de Enciso. Like many of the Spanish *conquistadors* of the day, Enciso had his eye on the vast riches that were said to be available in the lands west of Hispaniola, which the Spanish called Tierra Firma.

The Spaniards believed that jewels, gold, and fabrics could be found in Tierra Firma (which we call Central America today). Also in abundance, it was said, were pearls. Men had returned from voyages with stories of *la Costa de las Perlas*–the Pearl Coast. In that place, the explorers reported, the shiny white gems were so plentiful that Indians picked them out of the water as easily as a wine maker might pick grapes from the vine. One such explorer was Don Rodrigo de Bastidas, who had returned from a voyage to the Pearl Coast some eight years before with a fortune in pearls. Martín Fernández de Enciso wanted a share of these riches.

As Enciso's **brigantine** sailed from Hispaniola, he did not know that the ship carried an extra passenger–a man named Vasco Núñez de Balboa.

Balboa had been a member of Bastidas's crew, but had not shared in the riches from that voyage. Despite this, Balboa had prospered in the first few years following his return from Tierra Firma. He had become a farmer, growing melons, peppers, and the Indian corn known as maize on his land.

But in recent years, the farm had not produced bountiful crops. By the time Balboa heard that Enciso was preparing to head west for the Pearl

Coast, he was deeply in debt. He wanted to go along on the voyage, but the law of Hispaniola prohibited debtors from leaving the island before they repaid the people they owed.

So Balboa hatched a clever yet risky plan. He sold grain from his farm to Enciso, making the supplies available to the captain in large wooden barrels. On the night before the voyage, as the grain was loaded onto the brigantine, Balboa hid inside an empty barrel, which was taken aboard the ship alongside the barrels containing grain.

Once aboard the ship, Balboa carefully slipped out of the barrel and hid by wrapping himself inside one of the ship's large sails. Once the vessel was out to sea, he emerged from his hiding place. He then presented himself to Enciso, offering to join the crew and take part in the expedition.

Balboa was certainly taking a chance. Under the law of the sea, Enciso would have been within his rights to toss the stowaway overboard.

But Balboa told Enciso that he had been to the Pearl Coast before and knew where to find the pearls. Enciso decided that Balboa could be a valuable addition to the crew, and the stowaway was welcomed aboard.

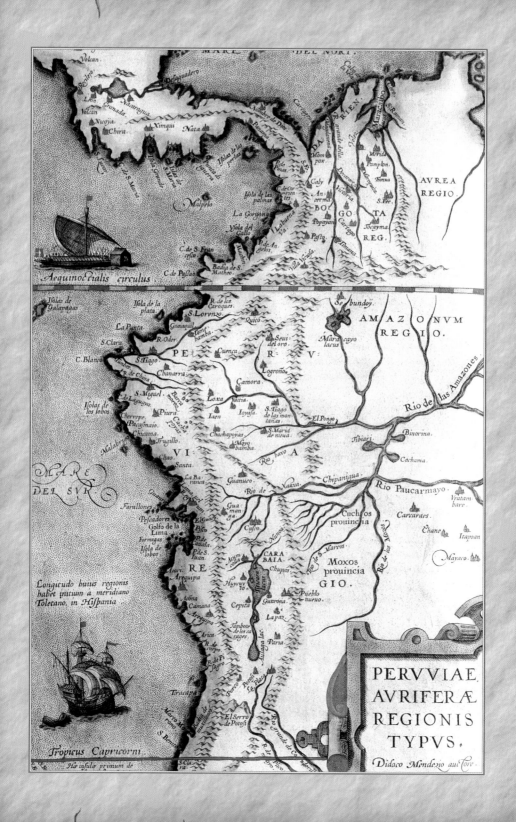

This Spanish map made in the mid-16th century shows Central and South America. The region that the Spanish called the Pearl Coast was actually the northern shore of South America, which is shown at the top right of this map.

The Pearl Coast

2

Christopher Columbus, an Italian explorer sailing under the flag of Spain, made four trips to the New World between 1492 and 1502. It was during his first trip in 1492 that he discovered Hispaniola. Today, the nations of Haiti and the Dominican Republic share the island.

Columbus's historic first trip in 1492 coincided with another important event in Spanish history. That year, the Spanish recaptured the city of Granada. This was the last stronghold of the **Moors**, warriors from North Africa who had crossed the Mediterranean Sea some 700 years before to make war on Spain. For many years, the Moors had occupied most of Spain, but beginning in the 11th century their power began to slip as Spanish armies started to slowly take back their country. Spaniards called this process the *Reconquista*, or reconquest.

Word of Columbus's voyage spread quickly through the newly unified Spain. The story of his exploits fell onto the ears of many brave Spanish soldiers and adventurers, who suddenly found themselves idle now that the Moors had been driven out of Spain. Many of them decided to pursue fortune and adventure across the Atlantic Ocean in the New World. During the next decade, explorers would sail from island to island in the Caribbean, planting the Spanish flag on Cuba, Jamaica, Puerto Rico, Trinidad, Martinique, and other islands. Today, many of those islands owe their language and culture to the early Spanish explorers.

Although the men who explored under the Spanish flag sought adventure, their main reason for joining expeditions to the New World was to make themselves wealthy. The Spanish explorers were conquistadors, men who conquered the Native Americans living in the New World. They then took their gold and jewels and made slaves of many of the vanquished natives.

On Christopher Columbus's fourth voyage to the New World in 1502, he sighted land in present-day Honduras. Columbus then traveled along the coast looking for a passage through the continent. He finally turned back to Hispaniola near an area the Spanish called Darién.

One of the men who longed for adventure in the New World was Balboa. He was born in 1475 at Jerez de los Caballeros, a town of some 14,000 people near the border of Portugal. His father was an *hidalgo*–a man of noble birth–but he was not wealthy. For this reason, his son had to find a job. As a youth, Balboa had mastered the sword, and his talents as a *fencing* instructor were very much in demand in Spanish society, because sword fighting was regarded as a valuable skill. Balboa was tall, blond-haired, and dashing.

It didn't take long for Balboa to find his way to the New World. Spain was alive with activity, as

King Ferdinand and Queen Isabella of Spain are pictured in the center of this illustration from a 16th century book. The monarchs had organized the drive to push the Moors from Spain, and supported Christopher Columbus's voyages west.

men made plans to follow Columbus's path and make their own discoveries. In 1498, when Columbus returned from his third voyage, he reported that he had seen Indians wearing pearl necklaces and had been told of the existence of the Pearl Coast, an area along the northern shores of what is today South America. That story fired the imaginations of many explorers, who dreamed of the vast riches that were waiting to be *exploited* in this far-off land.

One of these men was Don Rodrigo de Bastidas. King Ferdinand and Queen Isabella, the rulers of Spain, had given Bastidas permission to lead an expedition to Tierra Firma. The king and queen told Bastidas to sail west in search of "gold, silver, lead, tin, serpents, fishes, birds and monsters."

Bastidas left in 1500, leading an expedition of two ships, the *Santa María de Gracia* and the *San Antón*. Balboa was aboard one of those ships. He would never again return to Europe.

Bastidas spent four months exploring about 200 miles of the Pearl Coast. Balboa made many trips ashore, *traipsing* through the dense South American jungle. During his marches inland, he met many Indians. Balboa and the other Spaniards traded with the Native Americans, exchanging *trinkets* they had brought from Spain for gold nuggets, rings, and

In Central America, Balboa became familiar with the natives' ways. He also learned how to communicate with them. Balboa knew that some of the Indians were fierce fighters who dipped their arrow tips in poison.

jewels. And they found pearls. The Indians showed them beds of oysters in shallow pools of ocean water; when the Indians pried open the shells they found the tiny but valuable gems inside. Bastidas kept all the pearls for himself. By the time the voyage ended, he had filled three iron chests with the gems. He had also amassed a large quantity of pure gold, keeping that treasure for himself as well.

Bastidas's ships followed the Pearl Coast to the Gulf of Urabá, near the border of modern-day Colombia and Panama. From there, they crossed the gulf and landed in Panama, which the Spaniards called Darién. When Balboa went ashore, he found the Indians there friendly and willing to trade.

Bastidas spent the remainder of 1500 and most of 1501 in Darién. Believing that the Indians knew where to find more gold and pearls, the explorer had intended to remain in Darién for a much longer period. But Bastidas soon discovered that he had a major problem: his ships were sinking! They had been attacked by **shipworms**, wormlike clams that burrow into wood. Both ships were infested with the shipworms, which had been making quick work of the planks and timbers that were holding the vessels together.

Although the Spanish conquistadors came to the New World seeking gold and glory, men like Balboa were just as happy to gather pearls on the northern coast of South America.

Bastidas headed for Jamaica, making the voyage in about four weeks. After the ships were patched, Bastidas decided to sail for Spain. But it was late December, a time of the year when the waters of the Caribbean can be rough. Bad weather forced the ships to dock at an island just off the coast of Hispaniola. At first Bastidas decided to wait out the weather, but he soon grew impatient. In February 1502, he gave the order for the ships to sail again.

It was a foolish decision. The weather was still too rough to sail. On the first day out, black clouds gathered on the horizon, and a storm soon swept across the ocean.

By early the next morning, the *Santa María de Gracia* was in trouble. The ship was taking in water.

The *San Antón*, the smaller of the two ships, came alongside the *Santa María de Gracia*. Bastidas ordered that his treasure chests be transferred to the smaller ship. Balboa was one of the men who carried out this order, hefting the heavy cargo as the ships pitched high atop the choppy waves. Soon after the men and treasure were aboard the smaller boat, the *Santa María de Gracia* struck some rocks and broke apart. By now the *San Antón* was also taking in water and was in trouble. Fortunately, the men managed to sail to a nearby beach, where the ship went aground.

They had landed back on Hispaniola, near what is today the Haitian capital of Port-au-Prince. The castaways were 200 miles from Santo Domingo. They had no choice but to walk back to the capital. After two long and difficult weeks, the Spaniards made it back to Santo Domingo.

After the shipwreck, Bastidas, Balboa, and the others faced a difficult march. They had to carry the treasure over rugged and rocky terrain and through swamps filled with insects. The Indians watching them from deep inside the jungles also made the Spaniards nervous. They were pleased to see Santo Domingo.

The reception they got hardly qualified as a warm homecoming. In 1502 Santo Domingo was in every respect a frontier town, with muddy streets, sailors and soldiers living in shacks and huts, and **roughnecks** hired by the local governor to keep order. When Bastidas and his weary, hungry, and bedraggled crew emerged from the jungle, they were met with suspicious eyes by the authorities in Santo Domingo, who decided to take no chances. They threw Bastidas and his men in jail.

The crew members remained locked up for more than a month. Eventually Bastidas was able to convince the island's new governor, Nicolás de Ovando, that his men had run into bad luck while at sea and were not pirates. Ovando released the men. Bastidas quickly gathered up his gold and pearls and returned to Spain.

But Balboa decided to stay. His knowledge of the Caribbean had impressed Ovando, who offered Balboa a grant of 30 acres of farmland on Hispaniola as well as 20 Indian servants to work the land. The former sailor accepted the offer, settling in for what he believed would be a leisurely life as a gentleman farmer on a tropical paradise.

San Sebastián

The Sambu River, pictured here in the early evening, looks much the same today as it did when the Spanish first landed in Central America some 400 years ago. This river flows near the area known as Darién, where an early Spanish settlement was established.

3

By the time Enciso sailed west, most of the islands of the Caribbean had been discovered and explored. But the lands further west remained largely a mystery. Columbus had landed on the north shore of South America in 1498; he returned to Tierra Firma in 1502, when he briefly visited Colombia. Bastidas visited the land that would become known as Panama in 1501. Another explorer who had spent time along the Pearl

Coast was Alonso de Ojeda, who had traveled to the region in 1499. Ojeda would return 10 years later.

When Columbus made his first voyage, the intent of the mission was to find a western sea route to the Orient, as China, Japan, India, and the rest of eastern Asia were called. On October 12, 1492, when the great explorer landed on a tiny island near the Bahamas, he thought he had fulfilled his mission. Later, he mistook Cuba for part of the Asian mainland. In time, though, Spanish explorers discovered that they were far from the rich trading centers of the Orient.

Since the time of the Venetian explorer Marco Polo in the 13th century, European merchants had traveled to the Orient over what had become known as the Silk Road. The Silk Road was not a particular road or trail, but the name given to several routes that linked Europe and the Far East. It was not an easy journey. Merchants had to travel hundreds of miles in large *caravans* over rugged mountain paths and through blistering hot deserts and dark and dangerous forests. They had to hire armed guards because bandits lurked behind every curve in the trail. They had to endure the sudden changes in weather that swept through the Euro-

This detail from a 14th century map shows Marco Polo accompanying a caravan following the Silk Road to Asia. The trip east was slow and dangerous. By the 15th century, European nations such as Spain and Portugal were searching for faster sea routes to the Orient.

pean and Asian continents. Just as dangerous was the political climate: since communications traveled so slowly, the merchants usually had little idea when the local prince or sultan might have decided that Europeans were no longer welcome in his country.

But the riches of the Orient made the trips well worth the trouble. Despite its name, the Silk Road was more than a trade route for silk, the soft and elegant fabric that was used to make clothes worn by the wealthiest of people. Other trade items that traveled along the route from the Far East to Europe ranged from gold and ivory to exotic animals and plants. Also bought and sold along the Silk Road were *spices* the Europeans coveted: nutmeg from Java, ginger and cinnamon from India, musk from Tibet. Jewels were also carried back and forth: diamonds from India, rubies from central Asia, turquoise from Persia, pearls from Ceylon. In China, European merchants discovered a great source of *porcelain*.

By the time Columbus set out in search of the western sea route, merchants were still carrying their goods back from the Orient in horse- or mule-drawn carts or on the backs of camels. The trip took years, and even the largest caravan could not carry many goods. It was believed that a single ship sailing between China and a European capital could ferry the loads of 100 caravans—and make the trip much faster. So the search for a sea route continued. But the brief visits to Tierra Firma by Columbus and Bastidas had failed to find the path to the Orient.

In 1509, a few months before Balboa hatched his plan to stow away aboard Enciso's brigantine, an expedition left for Tierra Firma headed by Rodrigo de Nicuesa. Nicuesa had been dispatched by King Ferdinand to explore the lands west of the Gulf of Urabá, in a region that is now Panama. Meanwhile, the Spanish monarch dispatched a second voyage, this one headed by Ojeda, whom Ferdinand appointed governor of a territory named New Andalusia. This was the land lying east of the Gulf of Urabá. Today, this is the nation of Colombia.

Accompanying Ojeda on the 1509 voyage as ship's pilot was Juan de la Cosa. Cosa had sailed with Columbus in 1492.

Ojeda landed at Cartagena on the north coast of Colombia. The area was known for its hostile Indians, but Ojeda exhibited a brash and foolhardy courage. He and Cosa led a party ashore and marched deep into the jungle, finally arriving at a large Indian

Balboa had offered to sign on as a crew member under Ojeda. Unfortunately, he had not been allowed to leave Hispaniola because of his debts. The next year, he snuck aboard Enciso's ship. Enciso had been asked by Ojeda to follow his expedition to the New World and to bring supplies to the settlement that Ojeda wanted to establish.

village. Suddenly Ojeda, Cosa, and their landing party found themselves in a fight. They were hopelessly outnumbered, and the attacking Indians cut them down with arrows dipped in poison. Cosa was killed in the attack, as were most of the other members of the landing party. Ojeda managed to escape, making his way back to the coast and the safety of his brigantine.

Soon, Nicuesa arrived at Cartagena aboard a ship. With him was a force of 400 Spanish fighting men. Nicuesa and Ojeda returned to the native village with this army. They wanted revenge for their earlier defeat. The Spaniards attacked at night, killing many men, women, and children.

After the battle, Ojeda and Nicuesa returned to

Ojeda had visited the Pearl Coast once before, in 1499, but he had found no riches there. He had explored the northern shores of South America, naming that region "Little Venice" because he found Indian houses standing on stilts to keep them above the swampy lagoons. Those homes reminded him of houses he had seen in the Italian city of Venice, a town of many canals. In Spanish, Little Venice is translated "Venezuela." The name given to the land by Ojeda remains in use today.

Cartagena. Ojeda intended to establish a settlement nearby, while Nicuesa decided to sail on in search of new lands and riches. Nicuesa would soon die at sea, the victim of a shipwreck.

As for Ojeda, he marched west from Cartagena and established a walled stockade overlooking the Gulf of Urabá. He named the encampment San Sebastián. Soon, though, he realized that the walled fortress was really a prison. San Sebastián was constantly surrounded by Indians, ready to fire poisoned arrows at the Spaniards as soon as they left the protection of the stockade. Unable to hunt or *forage* for food outside the fortress walls, the men inside suffered from hunger and disease. Of the 300 men who helped build the walls of San Sebastián, 240 would be dead by the time Ojeda abandoned the fort and sailed back to Hispaniola. Ojeda died in Santo Domingo a short time later.

About 30 men chose to remain on the mainland to await Enciso, who was on the way with fresh supplies. When Enciso arrived in early 1510, he met the survivors some miles from San Sebastián, making camp on a beach. The survivors were weary, half-starved men under the command of a young soldier named Francisco Pizarro. In later years, Pizarro would go on to make his fortune—and earn his place in history—by conquering the Inca people of Peru. But now he was a hungry, sick soldier who had done his best to keep the San Sebastián settlers alive.

The survivors boarded one of Enciso's three ships. Unfortunately, they soon met misfortune when the brigantine ran into a sandbar in shallow waters just off the coast of South America. The ship broke apart. Supplies and weapons fell overboard, livestock drowned, and the men had to jump for their lives and swim to shore. They were able to salvage only a few barrels of flour and cheese.

Balboa met Francisco Pizarro in 1510, when he was in charge of a group of soldiers at San Sebastián. Pizarro and Balboa would become friends and work together in Darién. Pizarro was the second-in-command on Balboa's greatest journey: to find the South Sea in 1513.

They trudged back to San Sebastián to find the stockade burned to the ground by the Indians. The Spaniards now had no shelter to protect them from the hostile Indians lurking in the jungle.

While waiting for the other ships to return, Enciso turned to Balboa—the only man on the expedition who had been to the region before—and asked where they could find safety. Balboa suggested they could cross the Gulf of Urabá and make camp at Darién, a land Balboa had explored with Bastidas some 10 years before. He promised Enciso that the Indians of Darién were not as warlike as those in Cartagena and did not use poisoned arrows.

When Enciso's two remaining brigantines returned, the Spaniards boarded and sailed to a village in Darién. Balboa led the soldiers ashore on a raid, quickly defeating the ill-prepared and poorly armed Indians and taking their chief, a man named Cémaco, prisoner.

Enciso decided to establish a settlement on the grounds of the Indian village. He named it Santa María la Antigua del Darién. Called Antigua, it would become the first successful European settlement established on the mainland of the New World.

After taking charge of the Spanish settlement of Antigua, Balboa led several journeys into the Central American wilderness. Balboa was willing to trade peacefully with the Indians, but he did not hesitate to use force if he believed it would help him gain gold.

Mutiny at Antigua

4

E nciso did not last long as head of the settlement at Antigua. He had been asked to head the voyage by Ojeda, and now that Ojeda had returned to Hispaniola, the 180 Spanish soldiers living at Antigua soon questioned his authority. Also, Enciso did himself no favors when he chose to keep most of the gold and jewels that the men had taken as plunder from Cémaco's village. The men told Enciso that he was no longer in charge of the settlement. In what is believed to have been the first town meeting in the New World, the 180 citizens of Antigua met and named Balboa their first governor.

Enciso was enraged. He regarded the actions of Balboa and the others as little more than a **mutiny**. He soon left Antigua aboard a brigantine that had arrived with fresh supplies. He returned to Spain, where he made plans to overthrow Balboa.

Over the next two years Balboa would lead expeditions of discovery into the wilderness of Darién and nearby lands. These would also be expeditions of conquest. While Balboa was always ready to make peace and trade with the Native Americans he met, he was also willing to fight Indian tribes who made it clear he was not welcome on their land.

The first expedition, which he led in the spring of 1511, made its way up the Caribbean coast of Darién from the Gulf of Urabá to Careta, a point some 100 miles from Antigua. The explorers found stark cliffs facing the Atlantic Ocean and rocky islands just off the coast. The Indians of Careta were friendly and willing trading partners.

However, Balboa and the Spaniards found themselves walking into a war between the Careta Indians and a neighboring tribe, headed by a chief named Ponca. Balboa helped the Careta Indians by attacking Ponca's village. To show their gratitude, the Caretas provided Balboa with guides, who led the Spaniards inland to the village of Comogre, where they found an impressive, walled palace.

In Comogre, the Spaniards were given a lavish welcome by the Native Americans, who treated them to a feast. Inside the palace, the explorers found a cellar stocked with large earthen jars that held wine made from yucca fruit as well as potatoes, maize, and palm fruits. They also found that the Comogre Indians did not bury their dead. Instead, they **embalmed** the bodies and hung them from the rafters of their homes, covering the faces with ritual

The natives Balboa met in Central America had treasures other than gold and pearls. This mask, which was made of a valuable stone called jade, was used in burial rituals. It is now displayed in a museum in Mexico City.

masks. Balboa and the other explorers received gifts of gold from their hosts as well as 70 slaves to take back to Antigua.

During the feast, a Comogre prince named Panquiaco told Balboa that he was willing to provide the Spaniards with guides to a mountainous region to the west at a "distance of six suns." From those mountains, the prince said, Balboa could look out over the sea. He also told Balboa that he would find boats sailing in the sea piloted by Indians from Peru, known as Incas. This was the first time any of the Indians Balboa had encountered in Darién talked of a sea to the west.

Balboa returned to Antigua that December and wrote a letter to King Ferdinand. He informed the monarch that he was now governor of the settlement. He also said that he had made friends with the Indians in Careta and Comogre, and that many expeditions could be undertaken in Darién because the Indians had promised to provide guides and supplies.

Finally, Balboa told the king of the possible existence of what he called the South Sea. "They say the Indians come to the house of Comogre by canoe from the other sea to trade their gold and that these people are of good conduct," Balboa wrote. "They tell me that the other sea is very good to navigate in canoes, being always peaceful, and does not turn wild as it does on this coast. I believe that in the sea there are many islands and pearls in quantity."

Ferdinand sent word back that he was delighted with the news and that Balboa should now regard himself as governor of Darién. He also told Balboa to lead an expedition to find the South Sea.

Balboa was not yet ready to search for the South Sea. Instead, in early 1512 he decided to explore the region south of the Gulf of Urabá. This was to be a river journey, made by canoe. Mostly, the explorers traveled through broad rivers and unforgiving swamps deep into the South American tropical rain forest. On this trip, as with most of the journeys undertaken by the Spanish conquistadors, the goal was to find treasure. In particular, Balboa sought to find the village of the Indian chief Dabeiba, who was thought to rule over a land beyond the rain forest. Balboa believed that Dabeiba owned great stores of gold.

Balboa and his men sailed a brigantine to the southern tip of the Gulf of Urabá, then boarded canoes to make their way down the León River.

Balboa and his men prepare to set out in canoes. They
used the small crafts while exploring rivers and swamps
to the south of the Gulf of Urabá in 1512.

They paddled their canoes along the León for some
30 miles, encountering many Indian fishing villages.
In most cases, Balboa and his men would stop at the
villages and help themselves to whatever gold they
could plunder.

By June, the explorers found themselves at the
junction of the León and Atrato Rivers deep in
Colombia. Balboa chose to sail up the Atrato, which
would take the expedition back to the Gulf of
Urabá. He found that the Atrato was a wide river

bordered by many inhospitable swamps. Balboa later described the river in a letter to King Ferdinand. "The manner in which this river must be navigated is by canoes of the Indians, for there are many small and narrow tributaries, some closed by trees, and one cannot enter except in canoes three or four palms wide," Balboa wrote. In Balboa's day, a palm was a unit of measurement equal to about four inches—roughly the size of the palm of a hand.

"After this river had been explored, boats eight palms wide may be made to employ up to 20 oars, for it is a river of great current and not easy to navigate even in Indian canoes," he continued.

Balboa also told the king he found large bends in the river, and off in the distance he could see mountains "so high as to be covered with clouds . . . the crest has only been seen twice, for the sky is continuously covered."

Balboa was describing the Cordillera Occidental Mountains, a range of the rugged Andes Mountains. The Andes begin in Colombia and run south for 4,500 miles through the present-day nations of Ecuador, Peru, Bolivia, Argentina, and Chile.

Balboa failed to find the village of Dabeiba, but he felt certain that a future mission beyond the Gulf of Urabá could be successful. Indeed, when he called a halt to the mission, he believed that his expedition was but a two-day march from Dabeiba's village.

Still, Balboa decided to return to Antigua. The Native Americans he had met on the way had told him stories that Dabeiba had an army of thousands of fierce warriors. They also said the chief was a ruthless *cannibal* who would torture his captives and feed them to his people. Balboa was accompanied by just a few men, and he feared that the expedition would be overwhelmed by Dabeiba's hostile Indian army. Despite this, the explorer was sure that Dabeiba's treasure could be obtained by a well-armed force of Spanish soldiers.

"Many Indians that have seen it say that Dabeiba has certain chests of gold each

The Spanish were among the best soldiers in the world in the early 16th century. Wearing armor and carrying sharp lances, swords, crossbows, and an early type of gun called the arquebus, the Spaniards usually were more than a match for the Native Americans they encountered. A small force of Spanish soldiers could defeat a much larger Indian army.

requiring a man to lift," wrote Balboa in a letter to King Ferdinand in Spain. He continued:

> This chief has a great collection of gold in his house and a hundred men continually fabricating gold. All this I know as dependable information because I am never told anything different wherever I go. I have learned this from many Indians, as well as from subjects of this Dabeiba, as from other sources, finding it to be true in many ways, putting some to the torture, treating others with love, and giving others presents of things from the castle.

Balboa never returned to the country south of the Gulf of Urabá. As for Dabeiba, in later years many Spanish explorers searched for the village of the wealthy chief, but it was never found. The chief with his great chests of gold was probably nothing more than a folk legend.

The South Sea

Vasco Núñez de Balboa gazes out over the waters of the South Sea—the mighty ocean we today call the Pacific—on the morning of September 25, 1513.

5

In January of 1513 Balboa wrote again to King Ferdinand. This time he outlined his plans for an expedition into the western wilderness of Darién. Balboa proposed that he lead a party of 1,000 soldiers so that he might "enter the country inland and pass to the other sea on the side of the south."

He promised Ferdinand that great riches awaited a conquering army. "In those mountains are certain chiefs who have gold in quantity in their houses," Balboa wrote to the king. "They say those chiefs keep it in cribs like maize because they have so much gold that they do not wish to keep it in baskets. They say that all the rivers in the mountains carry gold, and that there are large nuggets in quantity."

Balboa wrote that if he had 1,000 men, he could "conquer a large part of the world." He also told the king he would need cannons, firearms, and other weapons, as well as ships. Finally, he outlined plans to build a number of forts in Darién.

> Perhaps Balboa believed he needed such a large force because he feared that the Indians of the west might be just as hostile as the Indians rumored to serve under the chief Dabeiba.

Unknown to Balboa, the king had also heard from Enciso, who had returned to Spain after being driven out of Antigua. Who was this Balboa, Enciso asked, this common crew member who thought himself worthy to command an army of 1,000 Spanish soldiers? In the 16th century, Spain was still very much a society ruled by men of noble birth. True, Balboa was the son of an hidalgo, but Enciso reminded the king that Balboa's family had little money, that Balboa had worked as a fencing instructor, and that he had stowed away aboard a ship to escape his debts. Although it was true that Ferdinand had appointed Balboa governor of Darién, Enciso reminded the king that Balboa had first come to power through what was little more than a mutiny.

Under the influence of Enciso, the king grew suspicious of Balboa's intentions. He decided to send a new governor to Darién. Ferdinand chose Pedrarias Dávila, naming him "our Captain and Governor of Tierra Firma." Dávila, a nobleman, knight, and friend of Queen Isabella, was dispatched to the New World with 1,500 soldiers under his command aboard a ***flotilla*** of 15 Spanish brigantines. When Dávila arrived in Darién, he was to begin an inquiry into Balboa's conduct.

Balboa decided that the only way to save himself was to offer the king a great accomplishment: the discovery of the South Sea. Balboa intended to find the sea and claim it in the name of Ferdinand. He launched the expedition on September 1, 1513, with 27 soldiers from Antigua and 800 Indians taken as laborers and guides.

The first leg of the march was over the familiar terrain that Balboa had explored two years earlier

The Spanish nobleman Pedrarias Dávila was sent by the king and queen to take over the Spanish colony at Darién. He arrived at the settlement while Balboa and his men were away searching for the South Sea.

when he was guided by the Indians of Careta and Comogre. After about a week of traveling, the troops hit unfamiliar ground. The soldiers had entered a swampy region known as Balsas. It took them four days to wade through the swamps and paddle canoes across the many rivers and streams they encountered. The Indian guides helped find paths through the murky wetlands.

On September 24 the party emerged from the swamps and arrived at an Indian village known as

Quareca. They found the natives living there unfriendly, and a fight ensued. Balboa and his men quickly overran the village, but they found little gold to take. Nevertheless, they asked captured Quareca Indians about the path to the South Sea and were advised to head south.

Balboa followed the path recommended by the Quareca Indians, and on the morning of September 25 he arrived at a small mountain ridge just west of the Sabana River. One of the Native American guides told Balboa that the South Sea lay just beyond the mountain ridge.

Balboa ordered the men to make camp at the base of the ridge. He wished to make the climb alone. Just after 10 o'clock in the morning, Balboa slowly made his way up the ridge.

He could see it! Below, the blue waters of what would later become known as the Pacific Ocean rolled peacefully along the western shore of Darién. He found himself peering down upon a gulf, which he decided to name the Gulf of San Miguel because he discovered the body of water on the day the Catholic Church honors St. Michael. After a few minutes, he summoned the other soldiers to join him. They ran quickly up the ridge, shouting, "The sea! The sea!"

"As the notices of another sea given us by the son of Comogre have turned out to be true, so will the words of Panquiaco be fulfilled concerning the riches of the lands to the south," Balboa declared. By that statement, Balboa meant that he intended to go on and explore Peru. There, he suspected, he would find great treasures in the hands of the Incas.

Back on the ridge, a priest named Andrés de Vara said a prayer, blessing the discovery of the South Sea. The men fashioned a cross out of timbers and set it upright in earth to mark the point of discovery. They carved the names of Ferdinand, Isabella, and other rulers of Spain on trees.

The men made their way down the ridge to the beach. In full armor, they waded into the waters of the Gulf of San Miguel. Balboa drew his sword and solemnly

In 1513, the length and breadth of the New World were still largely unknown to Europeans. A handful of explorers had been to Darién and points south. No one had yet landed in territory north of Darién. Francisco Fernández de Córdoba would make a brief visit to Mexico in 1517. Two years later, Hernando Cortés would lead a large army into Mexico and conquer the Aztecs.

Balboa, followed by his men, wades into the South Sea on September 25, 1513.

took possession of the South Sea in the name of King Ferdinand.

Because Europeans had barely explored the lands north and south of Darién, Balboa did not know that when he crossed Darién he had actually crossed an ***isthmus***—a narrow stretch of land across the water that links two large landmasses. Indeed, at its narrowest point, Panama is less than 50 miles wide.

Balboa's journey did not end at the shore of the South Sea. The expedition followed the coastline southeast to the Indian village of Chape. The men remained in the village for two weeks. The Chape Indians acted as guides, helping the Spaniards

The South Sea

Why did Balboa call the Pacific the "South" Sea? We usually think of the Pacific as being to the west of the Atlantic Ocean and the Caribbean Sea.

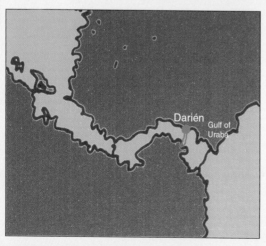

However, as the map at left shows, Balboa and his men traveled south from Darién, crossing Panama to reach the great ocean.

explore the territory and taking some soldiers on canoe trips into the Gulf of San Miguel. In the gulf, the Spaniards found many small islands, which Balboa named the Pearl *Archipelago*. Throughout the archipelago, the Chape Indians showed the explorers many oyster beds, rich with pearls. Balboa named the largest of the Pearl Islands "Rich Island," because the island's oyster beds were so filled with pearls.

Finally, in late October, Balboa decided to return to Antigua. The men carried home a treasure of gold they had plundered from the Indians and pearls they had found in the shallow waters of the Gulf of San Miguel.

Surely, Balboa thought, King Ferdinand would bestow honors on him for delivering to the Spanish empire the prize of the South Sea.

He couldn't have been more mistaken.

It would not be until the 20th century that the Panama Canal, part of which is shown here, would provide the short passage through the continent that 16th century mariners like Columbus and explorers like Balboa had hoped to find.

Route to the Pacific

6

Balboa's trip across the isthmus proved there was a South Sea. But he failed to find a navigable water route connecting the two oceans. There was none.

Hernando Cortés, who would conquer Mexico a few years later, was the first to suggest that a waterway could be built to connect the two oceans. He believed that a canal could be dug across the isthmus. But the engineers of the day did not have the technology or tools to undertake such a massive project. Not until 1881, under French direction, would a canal through Panama be attempted. But the French effort failed. The United States resumed work on the canal in 1904, and the Panama Canal was finally completed in 1914.

The South Sea was eventually named the Pacific Ocean by the Portuguese sea captain Ferdinand Magellan. "Pacific" means peaceful, and Magellan decided this perfectly suited the newly discovered ocean, because its waters seemed much calmer than the waves of the Atlantic. Magellan became the first European to sail across the Pacific, the world's largest ocean, in an expedition launched in 1519.

For the next four centuries, ships sailing west from Europe were forced to follow Magellan's route to the Pacific: they had to journey far south to sail around South America, then head north and west to the Orient.

❧❧❧❧❧❧

Dávila arrived at Darién in early 1514, leading a force of 1,500 soldiers. He found Antigua more than just a frontier outpost. Under Balboa, the settlement had grown into a bustling capital of the New World, where merchants, traders, carpenters, blacksmiths, leather workers, and tailors had flocked, no doubt drawn to Tierra Firma by stories of the land's bountiful gold and pearls. In fact, when Dávila arrived he announced that Darién would now have a new

The tough Portuguese sailor Ferdinand Magellan gave the Pacific its name during his voyage around the world from 1519 to 1522. Magellan, sailing for Spain, discovered a route from the Atlantic into the Pacific by sailing through a narrow passage near the southern tip of South America.

name: *Castillo del Oro.* (In English, this means "the Golden Castle.")

Civilization had come to the New World. The Catholic Church appointed Friar Juan de Quevedo the first bishop in Tierra Firma. Meanwhile, Dávila named Gaspar de Espinosa the **alcalde**, or mayor, of Antigua.

But what to do with Balboa, who had arrived on January 18, 1514, with his men? Dávila had been ordered by the king to inquire into Balboa's affairs, and determine whether he had led the mutiny that deposed Enciso. But Dávila's attention was quickly diverted by skirmishes taking place between the settlers and a group of Indians led by a chief named Tumanama, who had long been hostile to the Spanish intruders.

The battles between the Indians and the Spaniards became known as "the War of the Bloody Shirts," because the Indians stripped the shirts off the Spaniards they killed and carried the garments into battle as flags.

The fighting lasted for months, and for a time it appeared that Tumanama would emerge the victor and overrun Antigua. But the tide eventually turned in favor of the Spaniards, and Tumanama was driven back into the mountains.

After the War of the Bloody Shirts, Balboa proposed an exploration of the South Sea, particularly the Pearl Islands. Dávila gave his approval.

It would turn out to be a complicated undertaking that would cost many lives and add little to the Spaniards' knowledge of the New World. Special boats had to be constructed on the Atlantic side of the isthmus, then taken apart and transported dozens of miles over the swamps and mountains to the Pacific side. It took months of work by craftsmen and carpenters at Antigua to cut down the trees, strip off their bark, and split the timbers so they could be fashioned into boats.

Thousands of Indians were pressed into service to carry the parts of the ships across the isthmus. As many as 2,000 Indians may have lost their lives during the dangerous crossing.

Instead of retracing the route he had taken the year before, Balboa decided to take an unexplored path across the isthmus. This turned out to be a mistake, as the trip took longer than expected. Finally, though, the expedition arrived at the shore of the South Sea, and the ships were pieced back together and made ready for the voyage.

At first, the exploration of the South Sea went smoothly. The ships sailed through the Gulf of San Miguel toward the Pearl Archipelago. But when the crews saw schools of whales, they feared the large sea mammals would attack their boats. The sailors *implored* Balboa to turn back. Reluctantly, he agreed.

When he returned to Antigua, Balboa found himself placed under arrest. Across the Atlantic Ocean in Spain, Enciso had continued to poison the king's mind about Balboa, complaining against the explorer in Ferdinand's court. Balboa found Dávila hostile to him as well. For months, Dávila had heard about a vast and wealthy Indian nation to the south:

Some of the ruins of Old Panama, the Spanish settlement
that Pedrarias Dávila established while Balboa
languished in prison. The city was raided and destroyed
by the pirate Henry Morgan in 1671.

the Incas of Peru. Balboa had made plans to lead an army south to take the Inca gold. Dávila feared that if Balboa succeeded in the venture he would gain immeasurable favor with the king, and Ferdinand might strip Dávila of the governorship and hand it to Balboa.

So he had Balboa thrown into prison. Years later, Balboa's lieutenant Francisco Pizarro would lead the march south and conquer Peru.

While Balboa sat in prison, two men from Antigua, Diego de Albites and Tello de Guzmán, led an expedition up the coast on the Pacific side of the isthmus. Soon they arrived at the hut of a poor fisherman in an area the Indians called "Panama," which in their language meant a place of abundant sea life. Dávila decided to move the capital of Castillo del Oro from Antigua to this region, which he named Old Panama.

Balboa remained in prison for five years. Then, in 1519, Dávila put the explorer on trial.

The trial was a farce. Balboa was charged with *treason* for leading the mutiny that had driven Enciso out of Darién. He maintained his innocence, but Dávila wanted to rid Panama of Balboa. Dávila commanded the judge to convict Balboa and sentence him to death.

In 1671, the English pirate Henry Morgan burned the city at Old Panama to the ground. The city was rebuilt about 10 miles from its original site. Today, it is known as Panama City, and it is the capital of the nation of Panama.

On January 12, 1519, at the age of 43, Balboa was led to the executioner's block. There he met his death by the headsman's ax.

Chronology

1475 Vasco Núñez de Balboa born at Jerez de los Caballeros in Spain.

1492 Christopher Columbus discovers the New World; the Moors are driven out of Granada, their last stronghold in Spain.

1500 Balboa sails to the New World as a crew member aboard a ship captained by Rodrigo de Bastidas. After returning to Hispaniola, he is given land by the governor, Nicolás de Ovando.

1502 Christopher Columbus sights Central America during his fourth voyage to the New World. He follows the coastline south for hundreds of miles, searching unsuccessfully for a sea passage through the continent.

1509 Rodrigo de Nicuesa and Alonso de Ojeda lead separate groups of Spanish soldiers to Central America. Nicuesa is ordered to explore the lands west of the Gulf of Urabá (present-day Colombia), while Ojeda is to explore to the east of the gulf (present-day Panama).

1510 Balboa stows away aboard a ship heading for Central America in September to bring supplies to Ojeda's party; helps rescue the Spanish soldiers, including Francisco Pizarro, who are beseiged at San Sebastián; the expedition's leader, Martín Fernández de Enciso, is forced to leave the mainland after a series of mishaps, and Balboa remains behind as the leader of the settlement at Antigua.

1511 Balboa leads an expedition to the north and establishes relations with two Native American villages, Careta and Comogre.

1512 Leads an expedition to the south, mostly in canoes, through present-day Colombia and the Isthmus of Panama.

1513 Begins the expedition to search for the South Sea on September 1; discovers the South Sea, which is later named the Pacific Ocean, on September 25.

1514 Arrested and charged with treason after the arrival of Pedrarias Dávila, the new governor of Darién.

1519 Executed on January 12, after being convicted of leading the mutiny against Enciso.

Glossary

alcalde–the mayor of a Spanish town.

archipelago–a group of islands.

brigantine–a two-masted sailing ship with square rigging.

cannibal–a human that eats the flesh of another human.

caravan–a group of travelers on a journey, especially through desert or hostile areas; a train of pack animals.

conquistador–a Spanish soldier of the 16th century who conquered the Indians of the New World.

embalm–to prepare a dead body so that it will not decay.

exploit–to unjustly use a person or develop a natural resource to gain personal advantage.

fencing–the art of attack and defense with a sword.

flotilla–a large group of ships or boats.

forage–to search for food.

hidalgo–a Spaniard of noble birth.

implore–to plead with; beg.

isthmus–a narrow strip of land connecting two larger landmasses.

Moors–Arab and Berber peoples from northern Africa who occupied much of Spain between the 8th and 15th centuries.

mutiny–a revolt or rebellion against a leader's authority.

porcelain–a type of fine ceramic that was originally developed in China.

roughneck–a tough, rowdy person.

shipworms–wormlike clams that can burrow into wood, weakening it and eventually causing it to collapse.

spices–any of various aromatic vegetable products, such as pepper or nutmeg, used to season or flavor foods. In the 17th century, spices were rare and highly valued by the people of Europe.

traipse–to walk, travel, or wander about.

treason–the crime of betraying or attempting to overthrow a leader to whom a person owes allegiance.

trinket–a small ornament or object that has little value.

Further Reading

Chrisp, Peter. *The Spanish Conquests in the New World*. New York: Thomson Learning, 1993.

De Angelis, Gina. *Francisco Pizarro and the Conquest of the Inca*. Philadelphia: Chelsea House, 2001.

Gallagher, Jim. *Hernando de Soto and the Exploration of Florida*. Philadelphia: Chelsea House, 2000.

Konstam, Angus. *Historical Atlas of Exploration, 1492-1600*. New York: Checkmark Books, 2000.

Lomask, Milton. *Exploration, Great Lives*. New York: Charles Scribner's Sons, 1988.

Mirsky, Jeannette. *Balboa, Discoverer of the Pacific*. New York: Harper and Row, 1964.

Riesenberg, Felix Jr. *Balboa: Swordsman and Conquistador*. New York: Random House, 1956.

Index

Picture Credits

HAL MARCOVITZ is a journalist for the *Morning Call*, a newspaper based in Allentown, Pennsylvania. He has written more than a dozen books for young readers. He lives in Chalfont, Pennsylvania, with his wife, Gail, and daughters, Ashley and Michelle.